CAMBRIDGE

W0396963

Official Cambridge Exam Preparation

FUN Skills

Student's Book 2

Claire Medwell • Montse Watkin

Cambridge University Press
www.cambridge.org/elt

Cambridge Assessment English
www.cambridgeenglish.org

Information on this title: www.cambridge.org/9781108677370

First published 2020

20 19 18 17 16 15 14 13 12 11 10 9 8 7 6 5 4 3 2 1

Printed in Dubai by Oriental Press

A catalogue record for this publication is available from the British Library

ISBN 978-1-108-67737-0 Student's Book 2 with Home Booklet 2 and Audio Download

Download the audio for all the activities in the Student's Book and Home Booklet from www.cambridge.org/funskillsresources

Contents

Map of the book

Unit	Topic	Skills focus	Can do	
1 **My school bag** page 6	School bags and contents	**Reading and Writing** Read short sentences and recognise key words Tick or cross to show if a sentence is true or false	Read and understand short, simple words and the names of familiar objects	Chant Think Big
2 **Fun in the park!** page 10	Leisure activities	**Reading and Writing** Read short sentences about a picture and say whether they are true or not	Understand basic descriptions of everyday activities	
Review Units 1–2 *page 14*				
3 **It's my birthday!** page 16	Birthday activities Prepositions of place	**Listening** Identify key words in descriptions of people and select the correct name for each person by drawing a line to connect them **Speaking** Give and respond to simple instructions using prepositions of place	Understand simple spoken descriptions Understand and follow spoken instructions to point at and place objects in a picture	Chant
4 **My favourite things** page 20	Favourite things	**Reading and Writing** Spell simple words correctly **Speaking** Respond to simple questions	Unjumble words to match a picture Answer questions with simple answers and respond to *Tell me about …* questions	Chant
Review Units 3–4 *page 24*				
5 **Let's go shopping!** page 26	Things you can buy	**Listening** Listen for and write numbers (1–20) Spell names	Understand and write letters of the alphabet when heard Understand and write numbers 1–20 when heard	Song Think Big
6 **Cool homes** page 30	Houses, rooms and furniture	**Reading and Writing** Read a text, then choose and copy words to complete sentences	Understand and copy simple words	Think Big
Review Units 5–6 *page 34*				

1 My school bag

1 Look at the photos. Talk with a friend.

1 How many school bags can you see?
2 What colours are they?
3 What colour is your school bag?

2 02 Listen and match the bags to the children.

THINK BIG
Which bags are good?

3 Look at Max's school bag. How many things can you name?

Max's bag

My bag

4 Draw three objects in your bag and write.

I've got ______________________ , ______________________

and ______________________ in my school bag.

5 Find out about your friend's bag.

What's in your bag?

I've got a ruler.

Me too!

6 Read, think and write.

1 ✓ It's in Max's bag. ✗ It's not in my bag.
It's ______________________ .

2 ✓ It's in my bag. ✗ It's not in Max's bag.
It's ______________________ .

3 ✗ It's not in my bag. ✗ It's not in Max's bag.
It's ______________________ .

It's a notebook!

1 Look at the photos. Talk with a friend.

What's this?

What are these?

It's a/an ...

They're ...

2 Listen to the chant and match the photos.

03

3 Complete the words.

Example post _e_ _r_

1 _ _ _ board

2 book _ _ _ _

3 _ _ _ puter

4 key _ _ _ _ _

cup

er

com

case

board

4 **Work with a friend. Give instructions and tidy your classroom.**

TIP!

Don't forget to say *please* and *thank you*!

5 **Look and read. Put a tick (✓) or a cross (✗) in the box. There are two examples.**

Examples

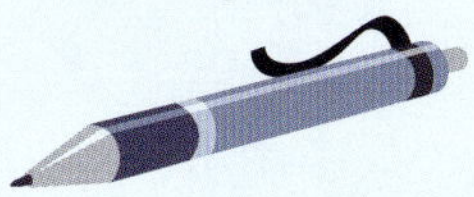

This is a pen. ✓

These are rulers. ✗

Questions

1  These are desks. ☐

2 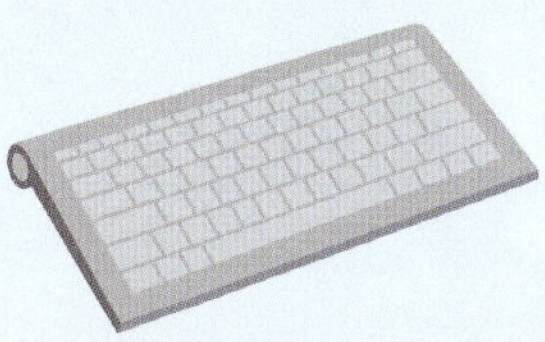 This is a cupboard. ☐

3  This is a bookcase. ☐

4  These are crayons. ☐

5  This is a poster. ☐

2 Fun in the park!

1 Look at the park for 30 seconds. What can you see?

2 Cover the picture and work with a friend. How many questions can you answer?

1 What colour are the bikes?
2 What animals are there?
3 How many children are there?
4 Where is the kite?
5 What sports can you see?
6 What's in the water?
7 What has the monkey got?
8 What is Frankie eating?

3 (04) Listen and circle the word you hear.

1	see	(bee)	3	bike	kite	5	dogs	ducks
2	sun	fun	4	boat	boots	6	bat	bag

4 Match the children to the verbs.

1 
2 
3 
4 

Grace   Ruby   Connor   Matt

throw   run   ride   kick

5 Look at the pictures in task 4. Listen and answer.

6 Write correct sentences.

Example Grace is holding her skateboard.

No, she isn't. She's *riding her skateboard* .

1 Matt is walking with his dog.

No, he isn't. He's ______________________________ .

2 Ruby is hitting a ball.

No, ______________________________ .

3 Connor is catching a football.

No, ______________________________ .

7 Imagine you are at the park. Do a mime. Can your friends guess?

1 💬 **Look at the park. Talk with a friend.**

1 How many animals can you see?

2 What are the animals doing?

2 👁 **Look and read. Write *yes* or *no*.**

Example A girl is walking with her dog. yes

1 The snake is holding an ice cream. ______

2 The crocodile is riding a bike. ______

3 The fish are sleeping in the water. ______

4 Grandpa has got a camera. ______

5 The monkey is flying a kite. ______

3 ✏ **What's in the photos? Find and write the words.**

1 t _ _ _

2 _ _ _ _ _ _ _

3 _ _ _ _

4 Read and choose the correct words.

5 What is good? Choose the correct picture.

A

B

C

6 Read the signs and match to the children in task 5. Write A, B or C.

1 ☐ Don't walk on the flowers.

2 ☐ Don't throw rubbish in the park.

3 ☐ BE NICE TO ANIMALS.

7 Make a word tree! Look at page 66.

Review Unit 1

Skills: Speaking, Writing and Reading

1 Talk with a friend. Look at the photo and answer the questions.

1 Where are the children?

2 Name four things you see in this classroom.

3 Name four things you don't see.

Mark: ___ / 9

2 Look at the photos and write the words.

1 Eva's bag is *orange*. It's in the ______________ .

2 Ben's bag is ______________ . It's on the ______________ .

3 Sue's bag is ______________ . It's next to the ______________ .

Mark: ___ / 5

3 Read and draw the things.

Example

a football in the bookcase

1 a computer on the desk

2 a mouse next to the computer

3 a ruler in the school bag

4 a clock on the bookcase

5 three crayons on the chair

Mark: ___ / 5

Total: ___ ___ / 19

Skills: Reading and Writing

1 Look at the photos. Write these words on the lines.

~~hit~~ kick ride run

1 
2 
3 
4 

1 hit
2 ____
3 ____
4 ____

Mark: ___ / 3

2 Look at the pictures and read the sentences. Write A or B.

A 

B 

1 A girl is riding a bike. A
2 A boy is catching a basketball. ___
3 A teacher is running. ___
4 Two ducks are swimming. ___

5 A dog is jumping. ___
6 A girl is throwing a toy. ___
7 A boy is flying a kite. ___
8 A girl is kicking a football. ___

Mark: ___ / 7

3 Look at the colours and write Frankie's sentences.

1

ball	window.	Don't	the	next to	the	kick
Don't	____	____	____	____	____	____ .

2

your	on	Don't	bike	grass.	ride	the
____	____	____	____	____	____	____ .

Mark: ___ / 6

Total: ___ ___ / 16

3 It's my birthday!

1 **Read and point to the photos.**

- **A** get a special card
- **B** open presents
- **C** play party games
- **D** wear new clothes
- **E** sing a song
- **F** eat special food

2 **Talk with two friends. What do you do on your birthday?**

I wear new clothes.

So do I!

I don't!

3 Can you guess what the presents are? Write the words.

1 

k i t e

2 

b ___ ___ ___

3 

r ___ ___ ___ ___

4 

t ___ ___ ___ ___

b ___ ___ ___

5 

l ___ ___ ___ ___

6 

b ___ ___ ___

4 06 Where are the presents? Listen and draw lines.

5 Draw a toy on a small sticky note. Look at the picture in task 3. Give instructions to your friend.

Put the robot in front of the chair!

between | under | next to | behind | in front of

1 07 Listen to the chant and draw lines.

Sara | Dan | Lucy | Tom

2 08 Listen and circle the correct words.

1 **She's / Her** name's Sara. **She's / Her** nine years old.

2 **He's / His** name's Dan. **He's / His** seven years old.

3 Ask and answer with a friend.

How old are you?

What's her name?

How old is he?

4 Draw and write about you and your friend.

This is ME!
My name's
______________________.
I'm ____________________
years old.

This is my friend.
____
______________________.
____
years old.

5 Look at the picture of a birthday party. What can you see?

6 09 Listen and draw lines. There is one example.

TIP!

There is one extra name. What is it?

7 Make a pop-up birthday card! Look at page 67.

4 My favourite things

1 Find and write Nedda's favourite things. Then listen and check. (10)

My favourite ...

colour rhymes with **new**. *blue*

animal rhymes with **frog**. ______

toy rhymes with **white**. ______

food rhymes with **snake**. ______

place rhymes with **tree**. ______

2 Read the groups of words. Circle the word that is not correct.

1	2	3	4	5
colour	animal	toy	food	place
brown	giraffe	bread	pea	pink
(bear)	goat	board game	pear	park
black	grapes	ball	paper	playground

3 Ask a friend about their favourite things.

4 Look at the pictures.
Look at the letters. Write the words.

TIP!
Use only the letters in the hearts.

Example

m a n g o

Questions

1 

_ _ _ _ _

2 

_ _ _ _ _

3 

_ _ _ _ _

4 

_ _ _ _ _ _

5 

_ _ _ _ _ _ _ _ _ _

5 Read and draw.

1 sweets on the cake
2 five peas on the ice cream
3 lemon in the lemonade
4 a monster in the story book

6 11 Listen to the chant. Draw the faces in task 5.

🙂 = like   ☹ = don't like

1 Look and write the words. Write one more question.

	Me	My frien
 1 Do you like p _ _ _ _ _ _ _ _ _ _ on your pizza?		
 2 Do you like big s _ _ _ _ _ at the zoo?		
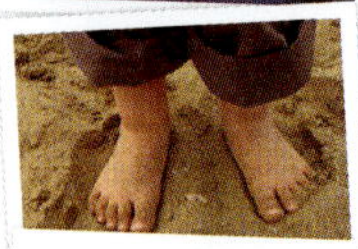 3 Do you like s _ _ _ under your feet?		
 4 Do you like f _ _ _ _ _ _ _ on TV?		
5 ____________________?		

Yes, I do! = 🙂 No, I don't! = ☹

2 Ask and answer with a friend. Draw the faces in task 1.

3 Talk about the picture with a friend. Take turns to ask.

1 What's this?
2 Where is the alien?
3 What colour are the alien's eyes?
4 How many birds are there?
5 What is the alien doing?
6 Tell me about the lizard.

TIP! It's OK to say: *Sorry, I don't understand. Can you say that again, please?*

4 Listen to the interview and circle the correct information.

1 The alien **likes / doesn't like** monsters.
2 The alien **likes / doesn't like** the sun.
3 Its favourite food is peas on **pizza / ice cream**.
4 The alien's favourite hobby is **flying / painting**.
5 It **likes / doesn't like** pink.

5 Draw and write about an alien.

My alien's name is ______________________ .

My alien has got ______________________

______________________ .

My alien lives ______________________

______________________ .

My alien likes ______________________

______________________ .

My alien doesn't like ______________________

______________________ .

6 Show your alien to your friends.

Review Unit 3

Skills: Speaking, Writing and Reading

1 **Look at the photos and talk with a friend. What can you see? What are the children doing?**

Mark: ___ / 4

2 **Read the text. Write these words on the lines.**

games He Her ~~my~~ eight too

Hi, I'm Sam! This is ___my___ friend, Bill. Bill is six years old. **1** ______ has got a sister. **2** ______ name is Suzi. She's **3** ______ years old. On Bill's birthday, we play **4** ______ and eat cake. We sing Happy Birthday! Bill likes birthdays. Me **5** ______ !

Mark: ___ / 5

3 **Look at the picture. Choose the correct word.**

Example The car is **in front of** / **next to** the robot.

1 The teddy bear is **next to** / **on** the table.

2 The cakes are **next to** / **in front of** the teddy bear.

3 The boy is **between** / **behind** the girls.

4 The toys are **under** / **on** the table.

5 The cat is **between** / **behind** the guitar.

Mark: ___ / 5

Total: ___ ___ / 14

Skills: Listening, Writing and Reading

1 13 **What are Lucy's favourite things? Listen and circle.**

A 
B 
C 
D 
E 
F 
G 
H 

Mark: ___ / 4

2 **Now write about Nick.**

1 Nick's favourite animals are 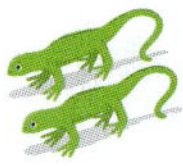 l i z a r d s

and  _ _ _ _ _ _ _ _ .

2 Nick doesn't like pizza. His favourite food is a  _ _ _ _ _ _ _ .

3 His favourite place is the  _ _ _ _ _ .

4 Nick has a red  _ _ _ _ . He plays with it in the park.

5 What is Nick's favourite colour? Yes, that's right, it's  _ _ _ _ _ _ .

Mark: ___ / 5

3 **Look at the picture and read the questions. Circle the correct answer.**

Example What animal is in the sea? — a fish / a lizard

1 What colour is the bird in the tree? — green / purple

2 How many children are there? — two / three

3 What is the boy wearing? — boots / a hat

4 What is he holding? — a boat / a fish

5 What is the girl doing? — jumping / swimming

Mark: ___ / 5

Total: ___ ___ / 14

5 Let's go shopping!

1 Talk with a friend. Name the things in the trolleys. Ask and answer.

Some crayons.

Trolley A!

2 Look at the trolley on page 68 for 30 seconds. Then write the words.

1 ______ 3 ______ 5 ______

2 ______ 4 ______

3 14 Listen and tick (✓) the letter you hear.

1 t ☐ d ☐ 2 p ☐ b ☐ 3 a ☐ h ☐ 4 i ☐ y ☐

5 f ☐ s ☐ 6 g ☐ j ☐ 7 m ☐ n ☐ 8 b ☐ v ☐

4 Write the first letters. Are the letters the same as in task 3?

1 
d olls

2 

_ ineapples

3 
_ ats

4 
_ ce cream

5 
_ ish

6 
_ eans

7 
_ eatballs

8 
_ oots

5 Student A: Look at task 4. Ask three questions. Student B: Close your book and write.

Can you spell ...?

How do you spell ...?

6 15 Listen and write the surnames.

1 
Layla _ _ _ _ _

2 
Robert _ _ _ _ _

3 
Captain _ _ _ _

A
12 eggs
_ mangoes
chicken

B
_ pies
_ kiwis
chocolate

C
_ eggs
_ limes
fish

7 15 Listen again. Match the people to the shopping lists. Write the numbers in the shopping lists.

1 Listen to the song and do the maths. How many sunflowers are in the flower shop?

20 – 5 = ☐ ☐ – ☐ = ☐

15 – ☐ = ☐ ☐ – ☐ = ☐

2 Complete your shopping list. Draw and write.

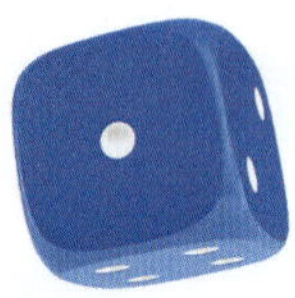

w

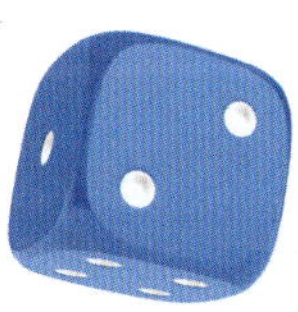

p

t

3 Play with a friend. Who can buy the things first?

I'd like a watermelon, please.

Here you are.

Can I have three tomatoes, please?

4 Read and point. Write the words.

We see numbers:

1 on a _ _ _ _ _ in our classroom. (k o c c l)
2 in a clothes _ _ _ _ . (h o s p)
3 on a _ _ _ in the street. (s u b)
4 on a birthday _ _ _ _ . (c e a k)
5 on the _ _ _ _ of a house. (o d o r)

THINK BIG
Where do you see numbers?

5 Read the questions in task 6. Say *name* or *number*.

6 Read the question. Listen and write a name or a number. There are two examples.

Examples

What is the boy's name? *Nick*

How old is he? *9*

Questions

1 What is the name of the street? ________ Street
2 What number is the shop? ________
3 Who is in the shop? Mrs ________
4 How many flowers does the girl want? ________
5 Who are the flowers for? ________

TIP!
All the answers are names or numbers.

6 Cool homes

1 ✏ **Write the questions. Ask a friend.**

1 do where live you?

______ ______ ______ ______ ?

2 rooms many are how there?

______ ______ ______ ______ ______ ?

2 💬 **Imagine you live in this tree house.**

1 What's good about your tree house?
2 What's bad about your tree house?
3 What animals live in the tree with you?
4 What furniture is in your tree house?

3 **Draw some furniture in your tree house. Talk about it with a friend.**

There is a big armchair.

There are lamps.

4 Can you complete the sentences? Read and write your ideas.

I live in a **1** __________ near my school.

There is a big kitchen, a dining room, a bathroom and three **2** __________ .

In my bedroom, there is a white cupboard with my **3** __________ . I've got a brown box with lots of **4** __________ . On the wall, there's a mirror and a poster of my favourite animal. It's an **5** __________ .

My ideas:

1 __________

2 __________

3 __________

4 __________

5 __________

5 (18) Are your ideas correct? Listen and write the words in task 4.

6 (19) Listen and point. Tell a friend what jobs you can see.

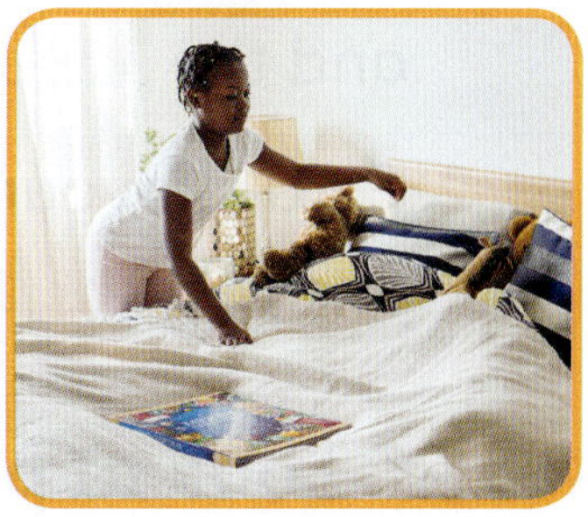

7 (20) Listen and match. Who's speaking?

1 Finn

2 Cara

3 Luke

4 Molly

A I make my bed.

B I put my toys in the toy box.

C I put things on the table for dinner.

D I clean the kitchen floor.

THINK BIG

What jobs do you do at home?

1 Talk with a friend. What can you see?

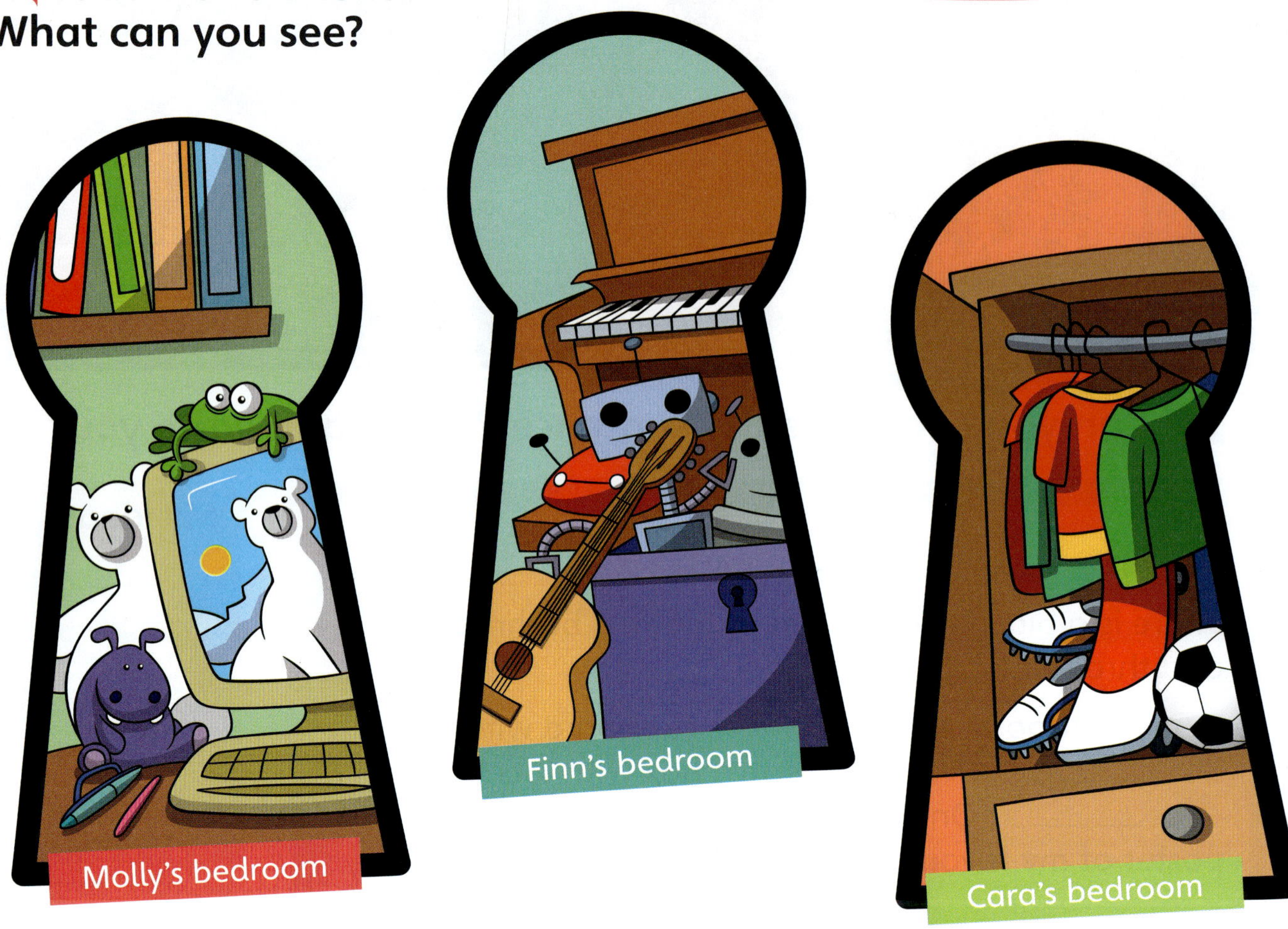

2 Read about Molly. Look and write about Finn and Cara.

Molly's favourite animal is the polar bear. She likes animals. She loves reading.

1 Finn plays the ______________________________
and the ____________________ . He loves playing with ____________________ .

2 Cara's favourite colours are ____________________ and ____________________ .
She plays ____________________ . She likes ____________________ .

3 Look at page 68. Draw three things in your bedroom. What do we learn about you?

My favourite ______________________________ is
______________________________ .
I like ______________________________ .
I love ______________________________ .

TIP!

Cover the pictures. Can you guess the missing words?

4 **Read this. Choose a word from the box. Write the correct word next to numbers 1–5. There is one example.**

Frogs

Do you like frogs? They are fantastic and cool! Frogs have four *legs* - two are long and two are short. Many frogs are green but some are grey or yellow. I like to sleep at **1** ________ but they like to sleep in the morning. Some people have a **2** ________ for a pet, but I have a frog! My frog doesn't live in my bathroom or under my **3** ________ . It lives in water in my **4** ________ . And my frog does not close its **5** ________ even when it sleeps! I love my frog!

Example

legs

night

garden

eyes

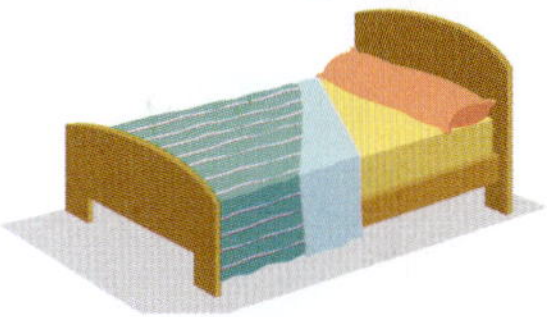
bed

apple

kite

dog

5 **Choose words to describe these houses. Which house do / don't you like?**

A

B

C

beautiful and scary	funny and silly	fantastic and cool

6 **Draw a house. Show your house to your class and talk about it.**

This is my house!

It's fantastic and cool!

Review Unit 5

Skills: Reading, Listening and Writing

1 Look at the people in the shops. Read and write the word.

I would like some *flowers*, please.

Can I have that red 1 ____________, please?

Here you are. A bag of 2 ____________.

Would you like a 3 ____________?

Can I have some new 4 ____________?

Mark: ___ / 4

2 21 Listen and write the number.

1

2

3

4

5

Mark: ___ / 5

3 Read the questions. Choose and write the answers.

1 How old is Pat? ____________

2 Who is your teacher? ____________

3 How many kiwis would you like? ____________

4 How do you spell your name? ____________

5 What number is your house? ____________

Seven, please.
W-E-B-B.
Mr Brown.
8 years old.
It's 15.

Mark: ___ / 5

Total: ___ ___ / 14

Review Unit 6

Skills: Reading, Writing and Speaking

1 Look at the house and number the rooms 1–5.

Example living room ___Room 5___

1 kitchen ______

2 bedroom ______

3 dining room ______

4 bathroom ______

Mark: __ / 4

2 Look at the house. Where are the people? Read the sentences and write the room.

Example Tom is sitting on the sofa. He's in the ___living room___ .

1 Grace is cleaning the cupboards. She's in the ______ .

2 Alex is putting things on the table for dinner. He's in the ______ .

3 Lucy is making the bed. She's in the ______ .

4 Mark is in the bath. He's in the ______ .

Mark: __ / 4

3 Look at the photo. Imagine this is your bedroom. Write the words on the lines.

My bedroom has got a big w _i_ _n_ _d_ _o_ _w_ . My **1** d _ _ _ is in front of the window. I haven't got a computer. There is a big **2** b _ _ _ _ _ _ _ with lots of books. It's next to my **3** b _ _ . My bedroom is very clean. All my **4** t _ _ _ are in boxes.

Mark: __ / 4

4 What's in your bedroom? Say two sentences to a friend.

Mark: __ / 4

Total: __ __ / 16

7 What would you like?

1 What can you see? Tell a friend.

2 Circle the food you can see in task 1.

a coconut	tomatoes	grapes	an orange
a pineapple	a pear	a mango	an onion
a banana	a potato	carrots	peas

3 Draw a person with some of the food from task 2. Show your picture to a friend.

Look at my picture.

I can see grapes.

4 22 Listen to the chant and say the letters. Then listen and write.

1 l _ _ _ _ _

2 o _ _ _ _ _ _

3 c _ _ _ _ _ _

4 t _ _ _ _ _ _ _

5 Making a cake! Listen and put a tick (✓) or cross (✗). Write the number.

	✓ / ✗	Number
bananas	✓	4
kiwis	___	___
carrots	___	___
eggs	___	___
mango	___	___
lemon	___	___
orange	___	___

6 Read and ask a friend.

This is my favourite fruit. Do you know its name? Can you see a star? It's a star fruit!

This is my favourite fruit. It's a very big fruit. It's a jackfruit. I like eating it with rice and coconut.

1 Do you want to eat a starfruit?

2 Would you like to eat a jackfruit?

Yes! No! Maybe!

7 Draw a picture and write about your favourite fruit.

This is my favourite fruit.

It's ______________________________ .

I like eating it with ______________________ .

1 Ask and answer with a friend.

What's this?

It's …

What are these?

They're …

2 Listen and number the pictures.

3 Listen and repeat.

This is the menu.

What would you like?

I'd like orange juice, please.

I'd like chicken with rice, please.

Here you are.

Mmm … thank you!

4 Write a menu.

5 Work in groups of three. Imagine you are in a café. Act out.

6 Ask and answer with a friend.

What's your favourite fruit / drink / lunch?

Do you like … ?

8 Let's have fun!

1 She's ______________.

2 They're ______________

3 He's ______________.

4 They're ______________.

1 **Talk with a friend. What's missing in each picture?**

2 **What are the children doing? Choose and write the words in task 1.**

dancing	drawing a picture	flying a plane	painting a picture
playing badminton	playing the drums	playing the guitar	singing

3 26 **Listen to Tom and circle the correct answers.**

Example

His favourite class at school is **doing sport** / **painting**.

1 His teacher is **Mrs Green** / **Mrs White**. She's really cool!

2 He likes painting **people** / **animals**.

3 Today, he's **drawing** / **painting** a cat in class.

4 His picture is **not good** / **fantastic**!

4 Write a question. Interview two friends.

Name		
What's your favourite sport?		
What do you like painting?		
Do you like singing?		
Do you like ______ ?		

5 Talk to your class about your friends.

Ben likes playing tennis.

6 Talk with a friend. What can you see in the pictures in task 7?

7 27 Listen and tick (✓) the box. There is one example.

What is Sam painting?

A ☐ B ☐ C ☑

1 What is Anna taking to school?

A ☐ B ☐ C ☐

2 What sport is Alice playing?

A ☐ B ☐ C ☐

3 What is Matt taking a photo of?

A ☐ B ☐ C ☐

4 What does Grace play?

A ☐ B ☐ C ☐

5 Which painting is Mark looking at?

A ☐ B ☐ C ☐

1 Look at the painting for one minute. Close your book. How many things can you remember?

There's a bed, a chair ...

2 Write these words on the lines.

behind	between	next to	~~on~~	under

Example There are five pictures *on* the wall.

1 There's a chair ______ the table and the bed.

2 There's a table ______ the mirror.

3 There's a picture ______ the window.

4 There are clothes ______ the bed.

THINK BIG

Three of these paintings are by a very famous artist. Can you find out his name?

3 Which paintings do you like? Choose words and write.

scary	funny	silly	beautiful	cool	fantastic

1

It's ______ .

2

It's ______ .

3

It's ______ .

4

It's ______ .

4 Talk to your friends about the paintings in task 3.

I like painting 2.

Me too! It's beautiful!

I don't! I like painting 1.

5 Look at painting 1 again. Read and write *yes* or *no*.

Example The man is playing a guitar. yes

1 There are a lot of people behind the man. ____

2 The women have got fruit in their hair. ____

3 The man is wearing a baseball cap. ____

4 The man is singing. ____

6 Choose and write words about painting 3.

beautiful boats ~~cloudy~~ green painting sand

It's a cloudy day. There are four **1** ____ boats on the **2** ____ . There is a red one, a **3** ____ one and two blue ones. Some more **4** ____ are sailing on the sea. I like this **5** ____ .

7 Play a game with a friend.

Colour the cool cat!

You need a dice.

1 Play in pairs.

2 Roll the dice.

3 Look at the number.

4 Colour part of the cat's body.

1 Colour the cat's head green.

2 Colour the cat's body yellow.

3 Colour the cat's big foot red.

4 Colour the cat's small foot blue.

5 Colour the cat's tail purple.

6 Colour the cat's back orange.

Review Unit 7

Skills: Listening, Writing and Speaking

1 28 **Whose lunch is it? Listen and match. Write *A*, *B* or *C*.**

Mark: ___ / 3

1 ☐ 

Max

2 ☐ 

Piper

3 ☐ 

Jesse

egg

1 ___________

2 ___________

3 ___________

4 ___________

5 ___________

2 What food can you see? Write on the lines in task 1.

Mark: ___ / 5

3 Which food do you like? Ask your partner two questions.

Do you like …?

What's your favourite …?

Mark: ___ / 4

4 Read the questions. Number the answers.

1 

Do you like bananas?

2 

Would you like a drink?

3 

What would you like?

4 

Here you are!

Mmm … thank you! ☐

Yes, please. I'd like lemonade. ☐

I'd like a burger, please. ☐

Yes, I do. They're my favourite fruit. 1

Mark: ___ / 3

Total: ___ / 15

Review Unit 8

Skills: Writing and Reading

1 What does Lucy like doing at school? Write these words.

doing sport | taking photos | ~~painting~~ | playing the piano | singing

painting

1 ____________

2 ____________

3 ____________

4 ____________

Mark: ___ / 4

2 Look at Lucy's painting. Write *yes* or *no*.

Example There's a bed under the window. yes

1 There are some pictures on the wall. ______

2 There's a bookcase next to the bed. ______

3 There's a cat on the bed. ______

4 There's a door next to the desk. ______

5 There's a rug in front of the bed. ______

Mark: ___ / 5

3 Answer the questions about Lucy's painting.

1 How many pictures are there? There are ____________ .

2 Do you like the painting? Yes, I ____________ . / No, I ____________ .

It's ____________ .

Mark: ___ / 3

Total: ___ ___ / 12

9 Let's go to the zoo!

1 Which animal is it? Talk with a friend and write the numbers.

bird	☐	elephant	☐	hippo	☐
lizard	☐	tiger	☐	zebra	☐

2 Read and colour.

1 red
2 yellow
3 black
4 white

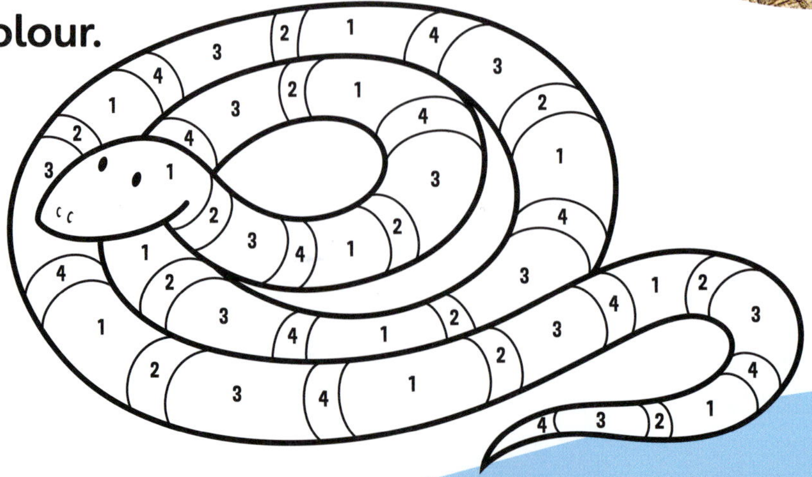

3 Look at the photos and choose the correct words.

1 I'm a **polar bear / hippo**.
2 I'm **white / grey**.
3 I've got **big / small** teeth.
4 I eat **birds / fish**.
5 I live in a **cold / hot** place.
6 I can **fly / swim**.

4 Look at the photos and write.

1 I'm a ______________________ .
2 I'm ______________________ .
3 I've got ______________________ .
4 I eat ______________________ .
5 I live ______________________ .
6 I can ______________________ .

THINK BIG
Some crocodiles are 5 metres long! How long is 5 metres? Find out!

5 Student A: Think of an animal. Student B: Ask three *yes/no* questions.

1 (29) **Listen to the song and number the pictures.**

A ☐

B ☐

C ☐

D ☐

2 **Answer the questions. Draw lines.**

1 Which animal is climbing a tree?
2 What is the giraffe doing?
3 Where is the tiger?
4 What is the tiger doing?
5 Which animal is throwing water?

A It's eating leaves.
B It's under the tree.
C the monkey
D the elephant
E It's sleeping.

3 (29) **Which of these words are in the song? Tick (✓) the words.**

1 zoo ✓
2 door
3 see
blue
four
shoe
you
me
tree
bee
too

4 (30) **How do the eight words sound? Put the words in groups 1–3. Then listen and check.**

5 Look at the pictures in task 6. What can you see?

6 Read the questions. Write one-word answers.

Examples

Where are the animals? in the *zoo*

How many animals are there? *five*

1 What is the boy looking at?

a ______________

2 Where is the balloon?

in the ______________

3 What is the monkey standing on?

the ______________

4 Who has got the balloon now?

the ______________

5 Is the boy sad?

no, he's ______________

7 Talk with a friend. Who helps the boy? Who can you help?

TIP!

Write only **one** word in your answers.

I can ______________ .

10 Fun on the beach

❶ 31 Close your eyes and listen to four sounds. Then open your eyes and tick (✓).

❷ Look at the photos in task 1 and write the words.

1 sea

2

3

4

5

6

7

8

3 Look at the photos in task 1. Answer with a friend.

1 Which things do you play with on the beach?
2 Which things can you see on the beach?
3 Which things do you find in the sea?

4 Talk with a friend. What do you like doing at the beach?

I like running on the beach.

So do I!

I like playing tennis.

I don't!

5 32 Listen and colour. There is one example.

TIP!
Learn the names of the colours.

1 Look at the pictures and tick (✓) the things on each list.

A Dan's towel

beach ball	✓
baseball cap	
camera	
apple	

B Eva's towel

kite	
camera	
bucket	
spade	

2 Write sentences about Dan and Eva.

Example Dan's got a *beach ball* .

1 Dan's got two ______ .

2 Dan hasn't got a ______ .

3 Eva's got ______ .

4 Eva ______ .

3 What do you take to the beach? Draw and show a friend.

I've got ...

4 (33) What does Dan like doing? Listen and tick (✓).

☑

1 
☐

2 
☐

3 
☐

4 
☐

5 
☐

5 (33) Listen again. Circle *yes* or *no*.

Example Dan likes flying a kite. **yes / (no)**

1 He plays tennis with his sister. **yes / no**

2 He's got a camera. **yes / no**

3 He doesn't like making sandcastles. **yes / no**

6 Make a sandcastle with Sam! Choose and write the words.

put	~~draw~~	make	find	take

Draw a circle in the sand.

3 ________ shells on the beach.

1 ________ sand in the bucket with a spade.

4 ________ a photo of your fantastic sandcastle!

2 ________ a big sandcastle!

7 (34) What does Piper say? Listen and repeat.

Skills: Reading, Listening and Writing

1 Look at the picture. Read and write *yes* or *no*.

Example A monkey is eating a banana in the tree. ___yes___

1 Two hippos are swimming in the water. ______

2 A zebra is running behind the tiger. ______

3 An elephant is standing in the water. ______

4 A giraffe is sitting next to the elephant. ______

5 A bear is catching a fish from the water. ______

Mark: ___ / 5

2 (35) Which animal is it? Listen and number the animals in the picture.

Mark: ___ / 6

3 What are the animals doing in the picture? Write five sentences in your notebook.

Example *The elephant is throwing water.*

The elephant
The monkeys
The giraffe
The snake
The hippos
The tiger

is
are

eating the tree.
swimming in the water.
playing in the tree.
running.
throwing water.
sleeping under the tree.

Mark: ___ / 5

Total: ___ ___ / 16

Skills: Speaking, Writing and Reading

1 Look at the beach and talk with a friend. What are the children doing?

Look! A girl is swimming.

Mark: ___ / 6

2 Write the names of the things in the picture.

1 b _o_ _a_ _t_
2 j _ _ _ _ _ _ _ _
3 f _ _ _
4 s _ _
5 s _ _ _ _ _ _ _ _ _
6 c _ _ _ _ _

Mark: ___ / 5

3 Read and draw the missing things in the picture.

1 A boy is flying a kite.
2 A girl is taking a photo of a bird.
3 A woman is eating an ice cream.
4 Two children are playing with a ball.
5 There are two shells on the sand.
6 There is a ship on the sea.

Mark: ___ / 6

Total: ___ ___ / 17

11 Our things

1 **Look at the picture. Answer the questions.**

1 How many children can you see?

2 What are the children doing?

2 36 **Listen to the song. Is the picture in task 1 correct?**

3 **Whose are the things? Look, read and choose.**

Examples  It's **Sara's** / **Jade's** watch.

 It's a phone. It's **hers** / **his**.

1  They're **Tom's** / **Jade's** glasses.

2  It's a bag. It's **hers** / **his**.

3  It's **Sara's** / **Jade's** baseball cap.

4  It's a jacket. It's **hers** / **his**.

4 37 **Listen and circle the words with the /ɪz/ sound.**

watches cameras sunglasses horses baseball caps sandwiches

5 38 **What can you see in the photos? Listen and number.**

6 **Match the sentences to the photos. Write A–F.**

1 We're walking in the forest. ___
2 We're listening to our teacher. A
3 She's eating her lunch. ___
4 We're giving food to the goats. ___
5 We're standing next to the school bus. ___
6 He's looking at the flowers. ___

7 **Talk with a friend. Where do you like going on school trips?**

I like this.

So do I. It's fun!

I don't! It's scary!

1 What's missing? Read and draw in the desks.

1

Hi I'm Diego! This is my desk. There are two **rulers**, some **pencils** and my favourite blue **baseball cap**. I've got a **painting** of this lovely butterfly!

2

Hello everyone! I'm Joel. There are lots of things in my desk. I have three **books**, a red **baseball cap**, **a tablet** and a **ball**.

3

Hello, I'm Hana. This is my desk. It's my favourite colour – red. I have a **book** to read, a yellow **baseball cap**, my **glasses** and this beautiful paper **ball**!

2 Point to the things in the desks. Ask and answer.

Whose is this?

It's Diego's.

3 Whose is this? Write *mine* or *yours*.

1 It's mine.

2 It's yours.

3 It's ______.

4 They're ______.

4 Draw four of your things. Ask and answer with a friend.

What's this?

Whose is this?

What colour is it?

5 Work in groups. Read the instructions and play a game!

1 Sit in a circle. Put your pictures on the floor.

2 Choose a picture.

3 Ask and answer.

12 What's your favourite game?

1 Look and write the words.

1 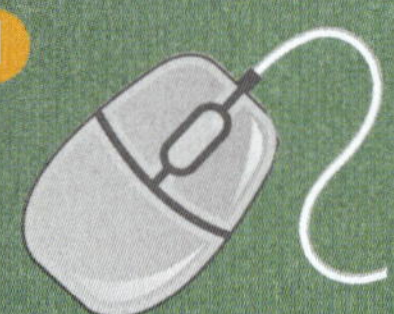

m o u s e

2 

k _ _ _ _ _ _ d

3 

w _ b _ _ _ _

4 

t _ b _ _ _

5 

g _ _ _

6 

c _ _ _ _ _ _ _

2 Look and talk with a friend. What are the children doing? Do you like these games?

A ☐ 

B ☐ 

C 1 

D ☐ 

He's singing.

I like this one!

This is my favourite!

3 39 Listen and number the pictures in task 2.

4 Look and read. Write *yes* or *no*.

Examples

The girl is holding her tablet. ___no___

There are four people in the room. ___yes___

Questions

1 There is an armchair next to the door. ______

2 The man has got the mouse in his hand. ______

3 The boy is singing. ______

4 The woman is looking at her tablet. ______

5 The dog is behind the sofa. ______

5 40 Listen and clap. Then say the chant.

Websites are fun!
Tablets are cool!
Computers are fantastic,
But playing tennis rules!

6 Write your own chant.

______ FUN!
______ COOL!
______ FANTASTIC,
But ______ !

1 Look at the photos and talk with a friend. What are the children doing?

1

2

3

4

THINK BIG

Which pictures show good ideas?

2 41 Listen and check your ideas. Which of these things do you do?

3 Choose words and write.

choose ~~open~~ play
read write

1

Open the app.

2

________ your name.

3

________ about the game.

4

________ a character.

5

________ the game!

4 Look at the picture and answer the questions.

Example What's the character's name?

1 What colour are his clothes?

2 What can he do?

3 Where does he live?

4 Where is he going?

His name is Captain Zoom. His clothes are green and
1 ____________ . He can 2 ____________ . He lives in a big
3 ____________ . He's going to the 4 ____________ in the sea.

5 Make a computer game character! Think about the questions and make notes. Then look at page 69.

1 What is your character's name? ____________

2 What does it wear? ____________

3 What can it do? ____________

4 Where does it live? ____________

6 Show your game to a friend and talk about it.

Review Unit 11

Skills: Listening, Writing and Reading

1 42 **What do Ann and Matt like doing? Listen and tick (✓) the photos.**

1 
2 
3 
4 

Mark: ___ / 4

2 42 **Listen again and circle Ann's things in red and Matt's things in green.**

Mark: ___ / 5

3 **Answer the question.**

Whose is the blue baseball cap?
It's Matt's / It's his .

Whose is the red baseball cap?
It's ___________ / It's ___________ .

Mark: ___ / 2

4 **Match the questions and answers.**

1 Do you like my photos?
2 Is this your camera?
3 Where do the children live?
4 How many children are there?
5 Are these your books?
6 What are you doing?

A In the country.
B Yes, they're cool!
C Ssshh! I'm listening to the teacher!
D No. They're Tom's.
E Yes, it is. It's mine.
F There are two.

Mark: ___ / 5
Total: ___ ___ / 16

Skills: Reading and Writing

1 Choose the words and write.

tablet | keyboard | mouse | ~~website~~ | phone

1 I **look at** the *website* .

2 I **read** on my ______ .

3 I **write** on the ______ .

4 I **choose** with the ______ .

5 I **listen** to music on my ______ .

Mark: __ / 4

2 Look at the game and choose the answers.

Example What's the character's name?

It's *Captain Zoom* / *Jesse.*

1 What colour are her clothes?

They're **beautiful / blue and pink**.

2 Where is she?

She's **under the sea / on the beach**.

3 What can she do?

She can **run / swim**.

4 Where is she going?

She's going to **the shell / boat**.

Mark: __ / 4

3 Answer the questions.

1 What's your name? ______

2 What are you wearing? ______

3 Where do you live? ______

4 What's your favourite game? ______

Mark: __ / 8

Total: __ __ / 16

Pairwork

Unit 2 page 13

7 Make a word tree!

1 Find leaves in the park.

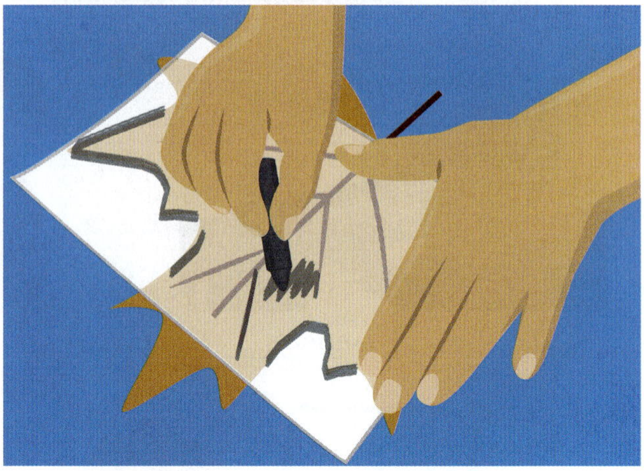

2 Put the leaves under paper and rub with a crayon.

3 Cut out the leaves.

4 Write your favourite park words on your leaves.

5 Make a class word tree.

Unit 3 page 19

7 Make a pop-up birthday card!

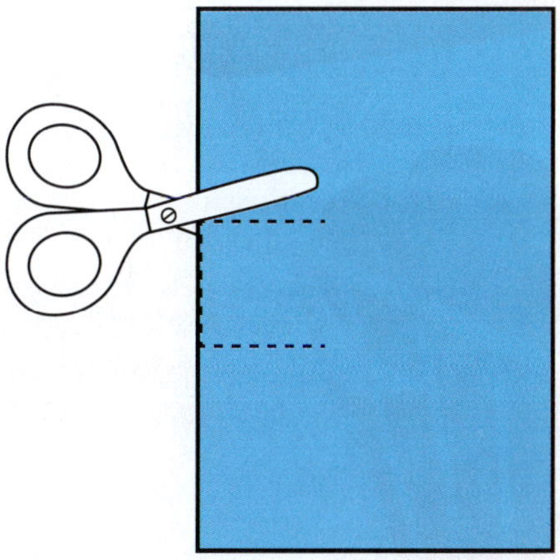

1 Fold and cut your card.

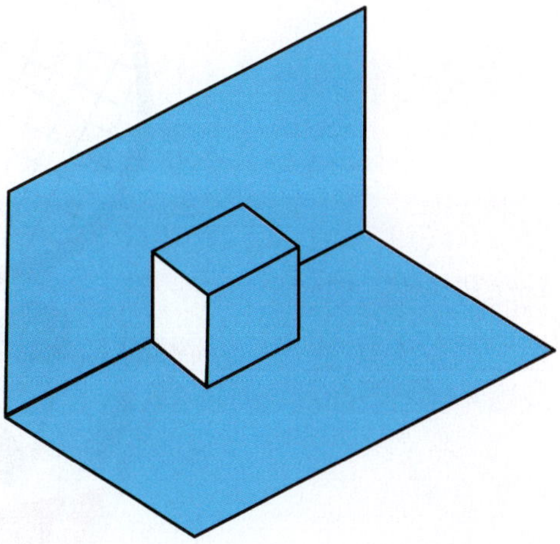

2 Open the card to make the box.

3 Draw your birthday picture.

4 Stick your picture on the box.

5 Write your card.

6 Give your card to a friend.

Pairwork

Unit 5 page 26

❷ **Look at the trolley. How many things can you remember in 30 seconds?**

Unit 6 page 32

❸ **Draw three things in your bedroom.**

What can you see in my bedroom?

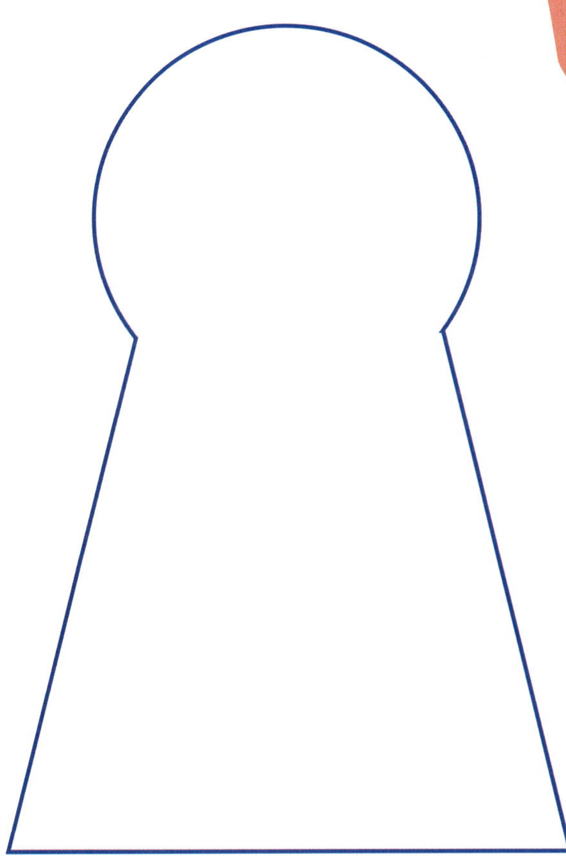

Unit 12 page 63

5 Make a computer game character! Draw and write.

START

1 Who is your character? Draw a picture.

2 What's your character's name?

3 What does it wear? Write.

4 What can your character do?

5 Where does it live? Draw your character's home.

Unit 1

Question words *what*, *how*, *who*, *how many*

What colour is your bag? **What's** in your bag? **What** do you do at school? **How** do you go to school? **How many** students are in your class? **Who's** your best friend?

what's = what is
who's = who is

1 Write the question words.

1 A: ________ have you got on your desk?
B: A book, a pencil and a ruler.

2 A: ________ is that boy?
B: It's Hugo.

3 A: ________ chocolates are there?
B: Ten!

4 A: ________ do you learn English?
B: I go to classes and read books.

Have got for possession

What **have** you **got** in your bag?	
Have you **got** a pen?	Yes, I **have**. / No, I **haven't**.
She **has got** / She**'s got** a cat. She **hasn't got** a dog.	

2 Complete the sentences. Use *have got*.

1 What ________ you ________ in your bedroom?

2 Ben ________ a teddy bear called Fred.

3 Q: ________ you ________ a helicopter?
A: Yes, I ________ .

4 Q: ________ she ________ a pet?
A: No, she ________ .

Unit 2

Imperatives

Walk on the grass. **Eat** your lunch.	**Don't walk** on the grass. **Don't eat** your lunch.

1 Match the sentences to the pictures.

1 Enjoy your food! ________

2 Be quiet! ________

3 Sleep well. ________

4 Close the window. ________

A

B

C

D

2 Complete the sentences with a verb from the box.

drink smile go show draw ~~bounce~~

Example Don't bounce the ball. (✗)

1 I'm tired. ________ to sleep! (✓)

2 ________ in my book. (✗)

3 Let's take a photo. ________ ! (✓)

4 ________ that juice. It's mine. (✗)

5 ________ me your drawing. (✓)

Grammar fun!

Unit 3

Question word *where*

Where are the presents?
Where do you meet your friends?

1 Match the questions to the answers.

1 Where does Tom sit?
2 Where do they live?
3 Where does Mark sleep?
4 Where is Sue?

A In a big bed.
B In the playground.
C In an apartment.
D At the front of the classroom.

Prepositions of place (*on*, *under*, *next to*, *in front of*, *behind*, *between*)

There's a teddy bear **on** the chair.
The mouse is **under** the sofa.
The sweets are **next to** the chocolates.
The bike is **in front of** the house.
The ball is **behind** the dog.
The monster is **between** the table and the balloons.

2 Write the prepositions.

Example

on

3

____

1

____

4

____

2

____

5

____

Unit 4

What (*a/an/–*) + adjective + noun

What **a** cool alien!
What **an** angry robot!
What fantastic shoes!

1 Complete the sentences with *What a/an/–* and the adjective.

1 ______________ pineapple! (nice)
2 ______________ hats! (beautiful)
3 ______________ hippo! (old)
4 ______________ room! (clean)
5 ______________ feet! (big)
6 ______________ monster! (ugly)
7 ______________ film! (scary)
8 ______________ clothes! (cool)

Unit 5

Determiners *a*, *the*, *some*

I've got **a** book. I've got **an** apple. I've got **some** books and **some** apples. What's the name of the street?

1 Choose the correct answers.

1 I've got **a** / **an** pet.
2 She's got **a** / **an** elephant.
3 They've got **a** / **an** question.
4 We've got **a** / **an** motorbike.
5 He's got **a** / **an** orange.
6 You've got **a** / **an** computer.

2 Complete the sentences with *a*, *an*, *the* or *some*.

1 Have you got ________ pen?
2 ________ ball under the chair is red.
3 There are ________ monkeys in the tree.
4 I want ________ apple.
5 I want ________ grapes.
6 ________ bus at school is green.

Unit 6

Present simple questions with *do* and short answers (*Yes, I do / No, I don't*)

Do you **like** frogs?	Yes, I **do**. / No, I **don't**.
Does she/he/the monster **make** her/his/its bed?	Yes, she/he/it **does**. / No, she/he/it **doesn't**.
Do they **clean** the floor?	Yes, they **do**. / No, they **don't**.

1 Put the questions in the correct order.

1 you / do / badminton? / play
____
2 like / she / music? / does
____
3 clean / does / he / bedroom? / his
____
4 photos? / do / take / you
____

2 Write questions.

Example (the robot / sing songs)
Does the robot sing songs?

1 (Abdullah / like pizza)
____
2 (Lucy and Kim / read many books)
____
3 (you / know the answer)
____

3 Answer the questions.

1 Do you walk to school?
________________ (✓)
2 Does the monster eat bananas?
________________ (✗)
3 Do Sofia and Matt like cheese?
________________ (✗)

Grammar fun!

Unit 7

Would like + noun or verb

I'd like a drink. She'**d like to eat** a starfruit.	
Would you **like to** eat a jackfruit?	Yes, I **would**. / No, I **wouldn't**.

I'd = I would
She'd = She would

1 Complete the sentences with *would like* and the noun or verb.

1 Anna ______________ . (an apple)
2 Nick ______________ . (eat chilli)
3 Matteo ______________ . (some new trousers)
4 Eva and Sam __________ . (swim in the sea)
5 __________ you __________ ? (come to my house)
6 __________ Ben __________ ? (a sandwich)

2 Answer the questions.

1 Would you like a drink?
______________________ (✗)
2 Would you like to take a picture?
______________________ (✓)
3 Would Lucy like to play?
______________________ (✓)

Unit 8

Adverbs: *really*, *very*

This painting is **very** famous.
She's **really** cool!

1 Put the sentences in the correct order.

1 doll / beautiful. / is / really / that
____
2 dirty. / is / bike / my / very
____
3 really / this / burger / good. / is
____
4 hair / long. / is / very / my
____
5 spiders / cool. / really / are
____

2 Add *very* or *really* to the sentences.

1 This watermelon is nice.
____
2 My skateboard is old.
____
3 That monkey is silly.
____
4 The jellyfish is scary.
____
5 My bedroom is clean.
____

Unit 9

Can for ability

Can you see? I **can** understand English. I **can't** see without my glasses.

1 Match the sentences to the pictures.

1 The baby can wave. ☐
2 She can't sing. ☐
3 He can play the guitar. ☐
4 He can't carry the suitcase. ☐
5 They can read Chinese. ☐

A 

B 

C 

D 

E 

Unit 10

Nouns: countable and uncountable

Countable Dan's got a beach ball. Eva's got two spades.
Uncountable Would you like **some water / rice / milk**? Would you like to listen to **some music**?
Irregular There are three **fish** in the sea! There are two **people / men / women / mice / children**. Cats have four **feet**.

1 Look and write. Use a number for countable nouns and *some* for uncountable nouns.

1 *some rice* 

2 *two apples* 

3 ______________ 

4 ______________ 

5 ______________ 

Can for requests/permission

Can I colour the jellyfish? **Can I have** some birthday cake?

2 Put the sentences in the correct order.

1 throw / ball? / the / I / can

____

2 some / have / water? / can / I

____

3 question? / ask / I / can / a

____

Grammar fun!

Unit 11

Possessive pronouns *mine, yours, his, hers, ours, theirs*

Whose watch is it?	It's my watch. = It's **mine**. It's your watch. = It's **yours**. It's his watch. = It's **his**. It's her watch. = It's **hers**. It's our watch. = It's **ours**. It's their watch. = It's **theirs**.

1 Complete the sentences with the correct possessive pronoun.

1 Is that robot __________ ? (you)

2 This is __________ ! (me)

3 That's not my classroom, it's __________ . (they)

4 I like my hat but I love __________ . (she)

5 This puppy is __________ . (we)

6 Those cats are __________ . (he)

2 Choose the correct answers.

1 I love your drawing. Do you like **my** / **mine**?

2 Is this jacket **your** / **yours**?

3 Do you like **our** / **ours** house?

4 **Her** / **Hers** bike is better than his.

5 **Their** / **theirs** dog is very small.

6 **My** / **Mine** favourite hobby is playing the guitar.

Unit 12

Conjunctions *and, but, or*

His clothes are green **and** yellow.
I'm big **but** I'm not strong.
Are you tall **or** short?

1 Make sentences.

1 A zebra is a fast runner

2 A horse doesn't eat meat

3 A frog can be green, yellow, blue

A but it eats grass.

B or orange.

C and it's black and white.

2 Write *and, but* or *or.*

1 The lizard is small __________ green.

2 Tigers are scary __________ I like them.

3 It's a small butterfly __________ it's beautiful.

4 My cat is black __________ white.

5 Eva likes football __________ tennis.

6 Monsters can be happy __________ angry.

7 I'm not thirsty __________ I'm hungry.

8 Would you like an orange juice __________ an apple juice?

Unit 7

Would like + noun or verb

1 What would you like? Ask and answer with a friend.

a drink	talk to a robot
a crocodile	have a pet
a duck	sing a song
a motorbike	go to a zoo
a kite	ride a horse

Examples
– *Would you like a drink?*
– *Yes, I would.*
– *Would you like to talk to a robot?*
– *No, I wouldn't.*

Unit 1

Question words *what, how, who, how many*

Student A

2 Ask a friend questions about Eva. Use *what colour*, *how*, *how many* and *who*. Write the answers.

Example
A: *What's her name?*
B: *Her name's Eva.*

Name:	Sam
Eye colour:	blue
Brothers:	2
Sisters:	1
Best friend:	Anna
Goes to school:	by bus

Name:	Eva
Eye colour:	
Brothers:	
Sisters:	
Best friend:	
Goes to school:	

Unit 3

Question word *where* & *prepositions of place*

Student A

3 Where are they? Ask a friend questions. Draw.

Listen to your friend and answer.
Ask about:

Piper
Frankie
Nedda

Examples
B: *Where is Piper?*
A: *He's in the garden. He's under the tree.*

Units 5 and 10

Determiners: *a, the, some*
Nouns: countable and uncountable

Student A

5 Tell a friend about the food.

Listen to your friend and draw.

Examples
A: *There's some orange juice.*

Grammar fun pairwork!

Unit 12

Conjunctions *and, but, or*

2 Add the conjunctions with a friend.

1 She's a good runner she can't swim.

____

2 He drinks orange juice apple juice for breakfast.

____

3 They like bears hippos.

____

Unit 1

Question words *what, how, who, how many*

Student B

3 Ask a friend questions about Sam. Use *what colour, how, how many* and *who*. Write the answers.

Examples B: *What's his name?*
A: *His name's Sam.*

Name:	Sam
Eye colour:	
Brothers:	
Sisters:	
Best friend:	
Goes to school:	

Name:	Eva
Eye colour:	brown
Brothers:	1
Sisters:	1
Best friend:	Grace
Goes to school:	by car

Unit 3

Question word *where* & prepositions of place

Student B

4 Where are they? Ask a friend questions. Draw.

Listen to your friend and answer.
Ask about:

Max
Frankie
Nedda

Examples **A:** *Where is Max?*
B: *He's in the bedroom. He's on the bed.*

Units 5 and 10

Determiners: *a, the, some*
Nouns: countable and uncountable

Student B

5 Tell a friend about the food.

Listen to a friend and draw.

Examples **B:** *There's some lemonade.*

Reading & Writing Checklist

Circle  if your answer is Yes!

My handwriting is clear and tidy.

I don't have problems spelling English words.

I can show if a word matches a picture by drawing a tick or a cross.

I know and can spell more than five food words.

I can answer questions about a picture with 'yes' or 'no'.

I can understand a short story with pictures.

I know and can spell more than five words for things at the beach.

I can write sentences about what people are doing.

I know and can spell more than five words for things in the house.

I can answer questions about a story by filling in gaps.

I knew the words for all the things in Max's school bag in task 3 on page 7.

I knew all the words in task 5 on page 9 and ticked and crossed the boxes correctly.

I wrote the sentences about the children in the park correctly in task 6 on page 11.

I wrote about me and my friend in task 4 on page 18.

I read the instructions and made a pop-up card in task 7 on page 19.

I unjumbled the words for places you see numbers in task 4 on page 29.

I wrote the correct words in the gaps in the text about frogs in task 4 on page 33.

I remember the six adjectives in task 3 on page 42 and I can spell them.

I wrote six sentences about the crocodile in task 4 on page 47.

I matched the sentences about the children on a school trip to the correct pictures in task 6 on page 57.

How many magic squirrels did you get?

Listening Checklist

Circle  if your answer is Yes!

I can recognise lots of words I know when they are spoken in my book.

I matched the names to the correct school bags in task 2 on page 6.

I like matching names to a picture of people by drawing a line.

I circled the correct answers about the alien in task 4 on page 23.

I can understand and write the numbers 1–20 when I hear them.

I pointed to the correct pictures of children in the house in task 6 on page 31.

I can choose the correct picture when I hear it described.

I put the pictures of the children in a café in the correct order in task 2 on page 38.

I can colour a picture when I listen to a description.

I circled the pictures with the correct colour in task 2 on page 64.

How many magic squirrels did you get?

Speaking Checklist

Check your progress, colour the stars!

	OK	Great
I can understand questions my teacher asks in English.		
I asked and answered questions about what is in a school bag in task 5 on page 7.		
I can talk about a picture using sentences, not just one word.		
I talked with my friend about what we do on our birthdays in task 2 on page 16.		
I can answer questions about pictures with short answers.		
I described my tree house in task 3 on page 30.		
I enjoyed acting out ordering a meal in a café in task 5 on page 39.		
I can speak about myself and what I like doing.		
I talked about the things I take to the beach in task 3 on page 52.		
It's fun to speak English in class.		

Word list

Unit 1

bag *n* ____________

blue *adj* ____________

classroom *n* ____________

colour *n* ____________

crayon *n* ____________

cupboard *n* ____________

desk *n* ____________

draw *v* ____________

green *adj* ____________

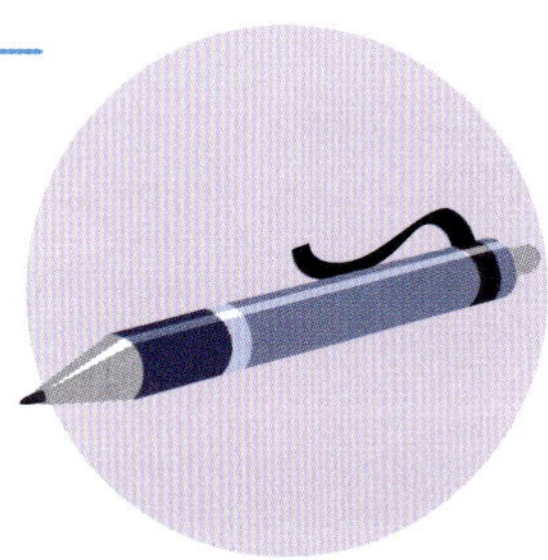

pen *n* ____________

photo *n* ____________

pink *adj* ____________

poster *n* ____________

purple *adj* ____________

read *v* ____________

ruler *n* ____________

school *n* ____________

talk *v* ____________

write *v* ____________

yellow *adj* ____________

Unit 2

ball *n* ____________

bat *n* ____________

bike *n* ____________

bird *n* ____________

boat *n* ____________

boots *n* ____________

brown *adj* ____________

camera *n* ____________

catch *v* ____________

clean *adj* ____________

crocodile *n* ____________

dirty *adj* ____________

dog *n* ____________

duck *n* ____________

eat *v* ____________

fish *n* ____________

flower *n* ____________

football *n* ____________

handbag *n* ____________

hit *v* ____________

hold *v* ____________

ice cream *n* ____________

kick *v* ____________

kite *n* ____________

monkey *n* ____________

paper *n* ____________

park *n* ____________

pick up *v* ____________

picture *n* ____________

ride *v* ____________

run *v* ____________

skateboard *n* ____________

sleep *v* ____________

snake *n* ____________

sun *n* ____________

throw *v* ____________

walk *v* ____________

water *n* ____________

Unit 3

balloon *n* ____________

birthday *n* ____________

cake *n* ____________

chair *n* ____________

clothes *n* ____________

open *v* ____________

robot *n* ____________

sing *v* ____________

song *n* ____________

toy *n* ____________

Unit 4

alien *n* ____________

beach *n* ____________

bear *n* ____________

bed *n* ____________

bedroom *n* ____________

black *adj* ____________

board game *n* ____________

book *n* ____________

bread *n* ____________

burger *n* ____________

ear *n* ____________

face *n* ____________

foot/feet *n* ____________

frog *n* ____________

giraffe *n* ____________

goat *n* ____________

grape *n* ____________

happy *adj* ____________

horse *n* ____________

lemon *n* ____________

lemonade *n* ____________

lizard *n* ____________

mango *n* ____________

monster *n* ____________

onion *n* ____________

orange *adj* ____________

paint *n* ____________

pea *n* ____________

pear *n* ____________

pineapple *n* ____________

plane *n* ____________

playground *n* ____________

sad *adj* ____________

sand *n* ____________

sea *n* ____________

shop *n* ______________

skateboarding *n* ______________

smile *n* ______________

spider *n* ______________

sweet(s) *n* ______________

tail *n* ______________

train *n* ______________

TV *n* ______________

watermelon *n* ______________

white *adj* ______________

zoo *n* ______________

Unit 5

banana *n* ______________

bookshop *n* ______________

bus *n* ______________

chicken *n* ______________

chocolate *n* ______________

clock *n* ______________

close *v* ______________

computer *n* ______________

doll *n* ______________

door *n* ______________

egg *n* ______________

glasses *n* ______________

grandma *n* ______________

hat *n* ______________

house *n* ______________

jacket *n* ______________

jeans *n* ______________

kiwi *n* ______________

lime *n* ______________

meatballs *n* ______________

nose *n* ______________

pie *n* ______________

potato *n* ______________

sock *n* ______________

street *n* ______________

teacher *n* ______________

teddy (bear) *n* ______________

tomato *n* ______________

T-shirt *n* ______________

Unit 6

armchair *n* ______________

bathroom *n* ______________

dinner *n* ______________

guitar *n* ______________

jellyfish *n* ______________

kitchen *n* ______________

mirror *n* ______________

piano *n* ______________

polar bear *n* ______________

scary *adj* ______________

tree *n* ______________

wall *n* ______________

Unit 7

breakfast *n* ______

carrot *n* ______

coconut *n* ______

juice *n* ______

lunch *n* ______

orange *n* ______

rice *n* ______

Unit 8

baseball *n* ______

basketball *n* ______

cat *n* ______

clap *v* ______

sheep *n* ______

shorts *n* ______

tennis *n* ______

window *n* ______

Unit 9

elephant *n* ______

fly *v* ______

hippo *n* ______

jump *v* ______

shoe *n* ______

swim *v* ______

tiger *n* ______

zebra *n* ______

Unit 10

apple *n* ______

baseball cap *n* ______

shell *n* ______

ship *n* ______

Unit 11

car *n* ______

cow *n* ______

pencil *n* ______

phone *n* ______

sit *v* ______

tablet *n* ______

watch *n* ______

Unit 12

hand *n* ______

keyboard (computer) *n* ______

mouse (computer) *n* ______

sofa *n* ______

In your book …

Nedda

Likes: puppies, videos, drawing, spaghetti, the moon, unicorns

Dislikes: sharks, lions, aliens, broccoli

Captain Zoom

Likes: sports, snow, skating, caves

Dislikes: water, dancing, umbrellas

Bobbie

Likes: carrot, music, eggs, apples, running, dancing, pears, grapes

Dislikes: candy, riding bikes, lettuce, oranges

Leon

Likes: friends, gum

Dislikes: blood, scary things

Piper

Likes: flying, reading stories

Dislikes: walking, hats, boots

Frankie

Likes: fashion, pink, bed, hugs

Dislikes: soup

… from kids around the world

Alejandra, 8

Hugo, 8

Julia, 8

Luíza, 7

Alan, 6

Anna, 7